ST ANDREWS CATHEDRAL

Stewart Cruden OBE, ARIBA, FSA

Formerly Inspector of Ancient Monuments for Scotland

Series Editor

David J Breeze BA, PhD, FSA, FSA Scot

Inspector of Ancient Monuments

Historic Buildings and Monuments

Scottish Development Department

Edinburgh

Her Majesty's Stationery Office

ST REGULUS CHURCH

Saint Regulus Church

The church of St Regulus is one of the most interesting of the early Scottish churches and its dating has been the subject of considerable controversy. It was the first church of the Augustinian Priory of St Andrews and the predecessor of the adjacent cathedral.

Founding of the Celtic Church

According to a legent embodied in later medieval chronicles St Rule or St Regulus, a Greek monk, was in the year 345 warned in a vision that the Emperor Constantine intended to remove the holy relics of the Apostle Andrew from Patras, where they were preserved, to Constantinople, the then capital of the Eastern Roman Empire. He acted upon the Divine revelation and accordingly, it is related, went to the shrine wherein they were kept and took thereof the arm-bone, three fingers of the right hand, a tooth, and one of the Apostle's knee-caps and set out with them to 'a region towards the west, situate in the utmost part of the world'. After a perilous voyage with a company of devout men and women he made a landfall on the coast near the present town of St Andrews where he is supposed to have erected a church in commemoration and thanksgiving for their merciful survival. What basis of truth there may be in this legend it is impossible to say. There are several variations of it and the story is confused.

It is also related that at the time Regulus landed a vision of the Apostle was revealed to Angus mac Fergus, King of the Picts, promising him victory over his enemies. Angus in gratitude for his subsequent victory dedicated the place to which the relics had been brought 'to God and St Andrew to be head and mother of all the churches in the Kingdom of the Picts'. The king and the holy men reverently made a circuit of the place, Regulus carrying upon his head the relics of St Andrew, his followers chanting hymns, while the king and his men followed them: round the consecrated ground they erected twelve stone crosses. By association with Angus the arrival of Regulus is brought down to a later and more probable date in the eighth century.

According to one interpretation of the 'Chronicle of the Picts and Scots', a later and more reliable source of information although still vague and defective in corroborative details, Angus II, son of Fergus, founded St Andrews in the ninth century. But the Irish Annals of Tighernach record the death of an abbot in 747 during the reign of Angus I almost 100 years before. A note appended to a copy of Wyntoun's Chronicle dated 1530 states that the relics were brought to St Andrews in 761, the year Angus I died.

We can accept Regulus as the founder of the earliest Christian settlement at St Andrews. It is probable that the holy relics were introduced by him during the reign of Angus I (731–61). During this period, in 732, Bishop Acca of Hexham, a well-known venerator of St Andrew, was banished from his diocese. His church was dedicated to

St Regulus Church seen through the door into the slype.

the Apostle. It too possessed relics of the Apostle. But both in dedication and relics it antedated the probable foundation of St Andrews in Scotland; for Hexham was founded certainly in 674 by Bishop Wilfred and the relics were brought there by Acca, his successor.

The coincidence of Acca's banishment suggests that the shrine of St Andrew was established in St Andrews in the middle of the eighth century during the reign of Angus I.

It is unlikely that the relics were corporeal. At this early period it was customary for them to take the form of pieces of fabric cut from the saint's apparel.

Striking evidence of close contact between St Andrews and Northumbria at this time may be seen in the collection of Early Christian sculptured stones displayed in the museum and hereafter described. They are of eighth- to tenth-century date and reveal strong Northumbrian influence on native work.

Whatever may be the truth obscured in these conflicting accounts of legend and defective historical evidence there is no doubt that the relics of the Apostle, real or supposed, were early held in St Andrews in great veneration and in a credulous age attracted devout pilgrims and enhanced the sanctity and importance of the place.

With the year 908 we are on firm chronological ground. In that year the only bishopric in Scotland was transferred from Abernethy, where it merely coincided with the royal residence, to St Andrews where it could profit by the presence of the miraculous relics. Nothing remains of the buildings of this early or Celtic period.

The Church of Rome

At the close of the eleventh century Anglo-Norman influence became dominant in Scotland. Malcolm III, 'Canmore' (1057/8–1093), had spend fourteen youthful years at the court of Edward the Confessor. His second queen was the saintly Margaret of the Saxon line, a refugee from William the Conqueror. Scotland was to her a foreign country and being by nature devout and trained in the ways and customs of the Roman Church of the continent, from which the Celtic church had for long been ritually severed, she proceeded, with her husband's help, to reform it and bring it into line with the Roman model. Turgot, prior of Durham, was chosen to be her spiritual director and Lanfranc of Canterbury her spiritual father. In 1107 Turgot became the first bishop of St Andrews of the new regime.

The time was otherwise ready for a change and after the accession of Margaret's sons, who inherited their mother's devotion, the movement was rapid and irresistible. As a result of the policy of fostering the church of Rome the ecclesiastical order in Scotland was refashioned according to the systematic remodelling general in Western Christendom. The old loosely-disciplined and reactionary Celtic or Culdee church was obliged to conform to the more highly organised and purposeful system of the Roman church by adapting itself to one or other of the regular monastic orders. The one preferred was generally the Augustinian as it was that which by its greater freedom from restraint and austerity most resembled the old order.

The Augustinian Order established in St Andrews

The first Augustinian house in Scotland was founded at Scone by Margaret's son, Alexander I, about 1120. It was colonised by six canons from the priory of St Oswald's at Nostell, in Yorkshire. It is recorded that Alexander, four months before his death in 1124, 'caused Robert, Prior of Scone, to be elected bishop of St Andrews'. He was consecrated in 1126 or 1127 and according to the thirteenth-century 'Legend of St Andrew', set himself zealously to accomplish what he had much at heart—the enlargement of his church and its dedication to divine worship.

Bishop Robert resolved to place canons in the church of St Andrews and would not suffer any of the Culdees to become inmates of the priory, by reason of the fact that they were a secular clergy and married men and could not therefore be expected to conform heartily to the self-denying ordinances of the canons regular. In the same year 1144, likewise as a precaution against future disunion, King David granted a charter to the prior and canons authorising them to receive the Culdees into the priory, with all their lands and possessions, should they be willing to become canons regular. Should the Culdees reject the opportunity of union they were to retain their possessions until death, after which the priory was authorised to appropriate them. Three years later the Pope deprived the Culdees of their right to elect the bishop and conferred it exclusively upon the canons of the priory and at the same time decreed that as they died their places were to be filled by canons regular. The suppression of the Culdees was slow, without violence, but persistent.

The Culdee church of St Mary of the Rock, of which the twelfth-century foundations can today be seen outside the precinct wall of the cathedral, to the north of it upon the cliffs overlooking the harbour, stoutly resisted the Catholic re-organisation. These monks continued to be intimately involved in the history of the cathedral in a manner now difficult to assess, although verified in documents as late as the fourteenth century, when their name disappears from the records.

The 'Legend' further testifies that by the time of the appointment of the first prior in 1144 the greater part of the church was in a state fit for occupation. Bishop Robert intended the priory to be the residence of the canons, 'men of moderate and contented minds who would wait with patience till better accommodation were provided'. He died in 1159 before this intention was realised, and the improved priory buildings, when built, were attached not to his church, but to its successor nearby, the cathedral of St Andrews.

St Andrews Cathedral, St Regulus Church and St Mary's on the Rock from the air. The whole extent of the cathedral precincts can be seen.

A LOFTY TOWER

The tower of St Regulus Church belongs to a type which there is reason to believe was common in England before the Norman Conquest. Similar towers, usually detached and near a later church, are found in North Italy. There is a close parallel at Wharram-le-Street in Yorkshire. The type is represented in Scotland at Dunblane Cathedral, Restenneth Priory, Muthill, Dunning and Markinch, as well as at St Andrews. They are all characterised by certain features of pre-Norman tradition and each, to a greater or less degree, has features which are distinctively Norman, but on architectural evidence alone it is difficult to date them with precision.

St Regulus Church consisted of a sanctuary and quire and lofty western tower. Nothing now remains of the sanctuary but the toothings of the side walls on the east face of the quire. It is apparent that a nave was not at first planned. The splayed base course, and the corbel-course which continues the wall-head line of the quire, both run round the western face of the tower as external features. That a nave was added at a later period may at least be inferred from the fact that the western arch of the tower enclosing the present entrance is a later insertion cutting through the corbel-course. But the identity of the moulded detail of this arch with that of the arches which undoubtedly belong to the original building proves that the insertion must be nearly contemporary. It may even have been made before the tower was completed and indicate merely a change of plan during construction. It is not impossible that this was the enlargement of the church which Bishop Robert 'zealously set himself to accomplish'. Higher up the wall face can be seen the chasing cut in the masonry for the housing of the roof timbers of the vanished nave.

The Chapter Seal, dating to the thirteenth century, drawn by T Borthwick.

The chapter seal, of which there are seven casts in the cathedral museum, ranging from the twelfth to the seventeenth centuries, shows a representation of a distinctly Romanesque church similar in some respects to St Regulus but inconsistent in others. It may be a stylised representation of a church of the period or an imperfect portrait of the actual building as it was in the twelfth century when the seal matrix was cut.

The tower is 32.9 m (108 ft) high. On the west front two flat buttresses rise to the corbel course. These appear to have been added, probably when the western arch was inserted, as the original splayed base

St Regulus Church from the east.

course of the walls passes through and behind them. The archway, which presumably replaces an earlier simple doorway, has twice been contracted, first in the thirteenth century and later in the sixteenth century. The jambs of the archway contain corner shafts capped by unusual capitals, similar to those in the quire and sanctuary arches and to those in the church of Wharram-le-Street, but not known in any other building in Scotland. The belfry of the tower is indicated by a string-course, serving as the sill of a double window on each face. The windows have had corner shafts and twin mid-shafts back to back which still remain. The double lights are topped by false semi-circular arches cut into the one lintel. Above each of the twin windows is a small doorway with an arched head. At the angles of the tower are putlog holes. Their purpose is not clear. On close inspection they prove to be cut through the masonry, as though a later structural expedient. They may be for the support of projecting timbers erected either as a constructional scaffold or a permanent overhanging gallery. The presence of the doorway and the occurrence of these holes only at the top of the tower strengthens the latter conjecture, although in the other similar towers in Scotland the disposition of the putlog holes is not so conclusive. At Dunning, Perthshire, for example, they occur in all five stages in height. The spire of St Regulus tower is shown on the seals as rising flush from the wall-head. The present wall-head and corbel course supporting it is of sixteenth-century date. The lower corbel course is original.

The blocked west tower arch of St Regulus Church.

On the eastern face of the tower are three raggles for a roof of which the middle is apparently the original. The highest may be of a thirteenth-century heightening, while the lowest is probably later, and may be that erected by Prior William de Lothian (1340–54). The eastern tower arch, like the western, is built up after being twice contracted. Above it is a small arched doorway giving access from the tower to the quire roof. It may be wholly or partly a later insertion.

In the sixteenth century the doorway in the south wall was forced through and at about the same time the present staircase was inserted.

The quire, unusually impressive in the small interior with its towering walls and arches and massive stone construction—all Saxon characteristics—is lit by two windows high in the north and south walls. These are widely splayed both internally and externally and have rounded heads externally cut through the lintel and internally formed of two courses dressed to arch shape and provided with a keystone. The archway between quire and sanctuary is at a higher level than the others, the sanctuary having been raised about 60 cm (2 ft) above the quire. The doorway in the north wall is a late insertion.

The general features described imply a general conclusion, that both St Regulus and Wharram-le-Street belong to a Yorkshire pre-Norman building tradition. A consideration of the peculiarities of the moulded detail permit a more certain conclusion. The capitals of the shafts are, in both buildings, of the same curiously elongated cubical type and have the archaic peculiarity of having a small roll necking worked not at the foot but above the bottom bed of the capital. On the other hand the distinctively Norman roll moulding, quirked on the external face and deeply recessed behind, is common to both buildings. The arch voussoirs at the springing are in both cases set too far back over the capitals and the arch curve is noticeably shaped like a horseshoe. The recessed orders are constructed in two rings, the inner penetrating behind the outer without a rebate or check. The joints of many of the voussoirs do not radiate correctly; they incline to points below the true centre of the arch. Some of these details are distinctly unusual and suggest a master-mason unfamiliar with the constructional principles involved in his building and with but a superficial understanding of the new Norman detail.

On the literary evidence, the church known today as St Regulus Tower was built between 1127 and 1144. In certain architectural features it so closely resembles the twelfth-century church of Wharram-le-Street, as to force the conclusion that the same school of Yorkshire masons was employed on both. There is an even closer parallel to be found in the church of Aubazine near Limoges in France, founded in 1135, with which both Wharram-le-Street and St Regulus may have an historical connection.

The documentary and architectural evidence, taken together, thus lead to the conclusion that sometime between 1126 and 1144 Bishop Robert, in order to build his priory church, now known as St Regulus, brought from Nostell in Northumbria a master mason who to a great extent followed the building tradition current there in pre-Norman times.

The south wall of St Regulus Church.

ST ANDREWS CATHEDRAL

The Cathedral and Priory of St Andrews is the successor to the adjacent church of St Regulus or St Rule.

The cathedral church had a dual function which it is necessary to appreciate for the proper understanding of its history. It was both the cathedral church of the diocese of St Andrews and the church of the Augustinian Order of Canons resident in the priory. The priory buildings were the domestic ranges attached to the church on its south side and were under the control of a prior.

Founding of the Cathedral

Bishop Robert, who founded the church of St Regulus, died in 1159. His successor was Arnold, abbot of Kelso, a Tironensian house. He, with the encouragement of Malcom IV, founded the great cathedral church in 1160 or 1161. The foundations were laid out to make it the longest church in Britain, with the exception of the cathedral of Norwich. According to the usual practice building in height began at the east end. We know that the quire was completed by 1238 as it is recorded that in that year Bishop Malvoisine was buried there. During his episcopacy all Scotland was laid under interdict for collaborating with the French—the 'Auld Alliance'—against the English, to his Holiness's displeasure. Bishop Malvoisine introduced the Dominican Friars into Scotland. The ruins of one of their houses may be seen today before Madras College in South Street. This house was founded by Bishop Wishart, in whose episcopacy (1273–79) the great west front of the cathedral church was wrecked in a storm. It was rebuilt by him where its stately but fragmentary ruins stand today. Wishart was bishop for nearly seven years and to him is attributed 'near al the body of the Kyrk', that is, almost all the nave. He was buried before the High Altar.

St Andrews Cathedral viewed from the chapter-house.

St Andrews' Bishops and the War of Independence

His successor was Bishop Frazer (1279–97) who advised Edward I of the rumour of the death of the Maid of Norway in 1290. Frazer was one of the plenipotentiaries proceeding, as he wrote, 'to Norway in order to treat with the Ambassadors from Norway for the due reception of our lady the Queen when a dismal rumour reached us that she was dead; a rumour that troubles and distracts the Kingdom of Scotland. As soon as Robert the Bruce heard of this he came to our meeting at Perth which he did not intend to do before. He is accompanied by a great retinue; but what his object is we have not yet heard'. With the death of the Maid a peaceful union of the two kingdoms was postponed for 300 years and a grandson of the Bruce, mentioned in Frazer's letter to Edward at a later date, made his object very clear to that same king. The Auld Alliance was renewed when Frazer was dispatched to France by Balliol on the occasion of his repudiation of his oath of allegiance to Edward. Frazer did not return to Scotland. He died in 1297 and was buried in Paris, in the church of the Preaching Friars, but his heart, encased in a very rich box, is said to have been brought home to Scotland by his successor, Lamberton, and entombed in the wall of the cathedral.

Lamberton consecrated the 'new kyrk cathedralle' in 1318, in the presence of King Robert the Bruce, seven bishops, fifteen abbots and a large company. Lamberton's election was the cause of a dispute which finally extinguished the expiring influence of the Culdee order in the nearby church of St Mary of the Rock. The election was contested by Edward I and the Culdees, but upheld by the pope, no doubt as much in order to curb the power of Edward as to increase that of Lamberton and his supporter Wallace.

Lamberton seems to have been a firm patriot. After receiving the support of Wallace, he made a treaty with Bruce in which they mutually pledged themselves to assist and defend each other against their common enemies 'under the penalty of £10,000 to be applied in prosecuting the war against the infidels in the Holy Land'. Shortly after this mutual assistance pact occurred the notorious murder of Comyn by Bruce and the subsequent excommunication of Bruce and his adherents. Notwithstanding the dangers incurred by displeasing both pope and Edward, Lamberton crowned Bruce at Scone in 1306. Edward urged the arrest of the bishop who had 'done him all the mischief in his power . . . and joined his enemies', and for this action and other infidelities he was seized and imprisoned with the bishop of Glasgow and the abbot of Scone. By order of Edward he was a prisoner in chains in the castle of Winchester for two years. To the pope Edward addressed a letter indicting Lamberton and dwelling at length upon the crime of perjury—of which this prelate had been repeatedly guilty—and requesting him to be deprived of office. This request was not complied with. Edward I died the following year. To Edward II Lamberton renewed his apparently uncertain allegiance. He swore fealty to him in 1308 yet in 1309 presided at an assembly of clergy at Dundee which vigorously asserted its allegiance to Bruce.

During those years of changing political conditions the war between England and Scotland was raging with great destructiveness. After Bannockburn Lamberton set about repairing the castle of St Andrews and adding to the priory. He erected a new chapter-house as an extension to the first and at his own expense. It was adorned with 'curious seats and ceilings'. The seats are the niches or wall-seats for the clergy, to be seen in the south wall. He presented to the canons utensils for the better celebration of their worship and provided the library with books. He also erected residences for himself and his successors at various places in Scotland and ten new churches in his own diocese.

His most notable achievement was the completion and dedication of the church, which, although attributed to Wishart, was after his episcopacy damaged by Edward I who stripped the roof of lead for use at the siege of Stirling. Lamberton died in the prior's chamber in 1328 after thirty eventful years of office.

The Great Fire

Some fifty years later, in the time of Bishop William de Landells, a great part of the cathedral was destroyed by fire. The chronicler Wyntoun, who was a canon of the priory at the time of the repair, informs us in his 'Orygynal Cronikil' that the timber work of the quire and cross-kyrk (transepts) had to be renewed and these divisions roofed with lead. 'Twa pillaris new' in each transept were also constructed 'as ye may see them appear—and under the auld work yet standand'. Nothing of the transept piers, old or new, now remains. It is recorded further by Wyntoun that one quarter (side) of the 'stepil of stane' was erected—ie presumably one side of a crossing tower—and that in the body of the kyrk or nave nine main piers were erected, counting eastwards from the west end, a major task of reconstruction embellished with the different coats of arms of the lords who had contributed towards the expense.

The most urgent work of consolidation took seven years to complete and the extensive damage was not fully remedied until 1440. So great was the task and so important the result that the pope, Clement VII, in 1381 authorised the tithes of many neighbouring farms to be allotted to defray the cost and liberal indulgences to those who would contribute thereto. Doubtless this encouraged the aforesaid lords to assist in the holy work of reconstruction. Landells provided the church and priory generously with fair jewels, vestments, books and other furnishings. He died in 1385, and was buried in the floor of the church before the door of the vestry or sacristy.

His successor-elect was Prior Stephen de Pay, with whom he had bravely undertaken the formidable task of rebuilding. Pay was captured 'by pirates' on his way to Rome for confirmation. Rather than burden his monastery with the cost of his ransom, more particularly after the expensive catastrophe of the great fire which he had done so much to remedy seven years previously, he preferred to remain in England, where he died, at Alnwick, soon after. His capture is described by Wyntoun in curiously modern war-phraseology:

He made hym to the court to pass
But in hot war the Inglishman
Had in the sea their bargis then, etc.

In 1409, during the episcopacy of Bishop Wardlaw—who founded the University in 1411—the south transept gable was thrown down in a storm, causing great damage. Meantime the nave, although covered, was unfinished until Prior James Haldenston (1419–43) provided it with windows of glass, altars, images and furnishings.

The head of a bishop—possibly Bishop Wardlaw—from a tombstone, probably formerly in the cathedral, but now in the museum.

In 1472 St Andrews was erected to the dignity of an archepiscopal and metropolitan see and for the next hundred years required only minor repairs. After the Reformation, when it suffered the 'burning of images and mass-books and breaking of altars', it was allowed to fall into decay.

In 1826 the Barons of the Exchequer took possession of the ruins of the cathedral. In 1946 the priory was given to the state by Major M D D Crichton-Stuart.

CATHEDRAL AND PRIORY

The Cathedral

Once the longest and greatest church in all Scotland, the cathedral is today a fragmentary but imposing ruin. When complete it was an aisled cruciform building with a central tower and a high unaisled and square-ended sanctuary of the type known as the 'canon's ending'.

The Sanctuary

The original twelfth-century east gable wall is retained, an unusual survival, and in Scotland paralleled only at the almost contemporary abbey church of Arbroath. It is 18·3 m (60 ft) high to the wall-head. The upper part of the gable has vanished but the roof-slope is determinable. On each of the corner turrets can be seen deep oblique chases in the masonry, evidence of the housing of the diagonal rafters. The large pointed window with the tusks of its tracery hanging from the arch is a late insertion by Prior Haldenston (1419–43). The original composition of the gable can still be seen in the existing masonry. The range of three round-headed windows is the lowest of three such ranges disposed one above the other. A careful scrutiny of the masonry both inside and out will disclose the indications. The upper tiers were blocked during the Haldenston reconstruction. These round-headed windows are of the first building period, in the Transitional or late twelfth-century style.

The east front of St Andrews Cathedral, viewed from the choir.

At the angles of the gable wall pilaster buttresses with angle-shafts rise to stop beneath hollow corbels at the wall-head. Against the north-east buttress a later and more massive buttress of fifteenth-century date has been added for support, probably when the sanctuary was vaulted. The corner springers or 'tas de charge' of this vaulting can still be seen. Other evidence of instability is apparent in the external patching-up of the north wall of the sanctuary near the large buttress.

A blind arcading of interlaced arches, similar to those in the south transept, ran round the sanctuary. These were doubtless removed by Haldenston and of them nothing remains but the bases of some of the shafts. The broken ends of the sanctuary side walls show the openings of the triforium and clerestory passages. The detail of the clerestory indicates that by the time height was reached the style had changed from late twelfth-century Transitional to thirteenth-century First Pointed. Access to the parapet walk was made by a wheel-stair and through a door in each of the corner turrets. The sanctuary was originally two steps above the quire level; in it stood the high altar.

The great slab of Tournai marble made to hold monumental brasses, and the stone coffins below, discovered in 1826, are not in their original positions. Beside them is a tomb, while another, unfortunately incomplete, lies beneath the eastern arch of the north quire arcade. A third was made in the north wall of the church and in the second bay from west end. This is a fourteenth-century insertion attributed

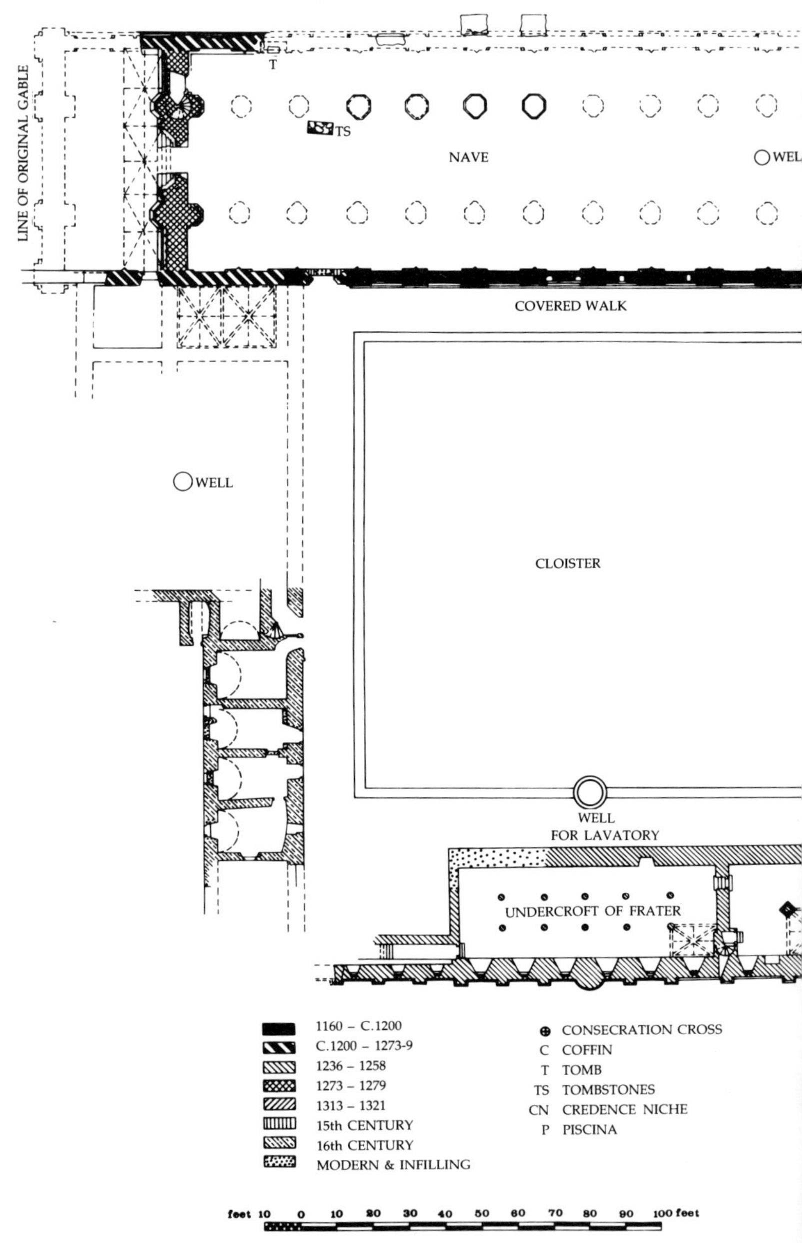
T
LINE OF ORIGINAL GABLE
TS
NAVE
WELL
COVERED WALK
WELL
CLOISTER
WELL
FOR LAVATORY
UNDERCROFT OF FRATER
1160 – C.1200
C.1200 – 1273-9
1236 – 1258
1273 – 1279
1313 – 1321
15th CENTURY
16th CENTURY
MODERN & INFILLING
CONSECRATION CROSS
C COFFIN
T TOMB
TS TOMBSTONES
CN CREDENCE NICHE
P PISCINA
feet 10 0 10 20 30 40 50 60 70 80 90 100 feet

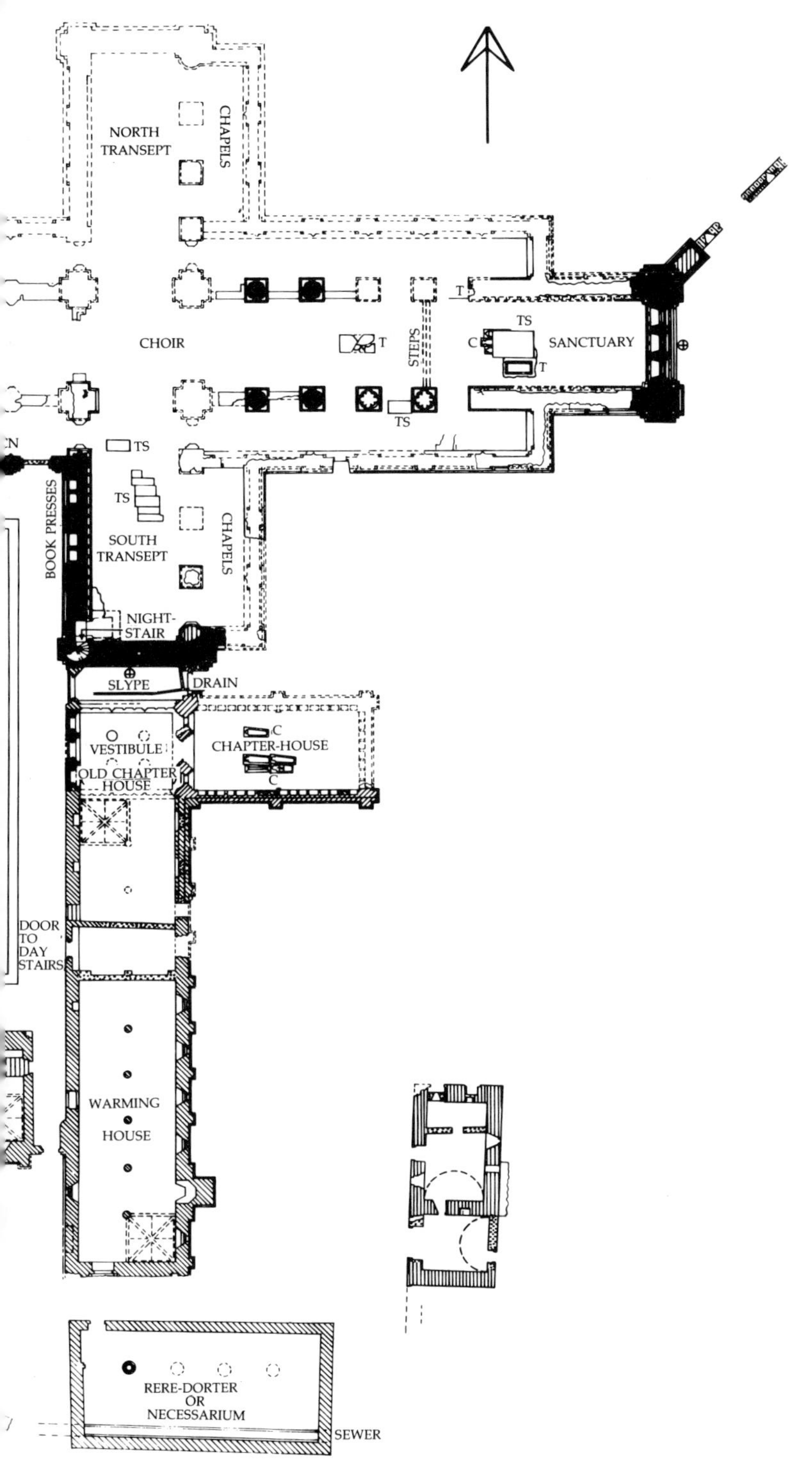
NORTH
TRANSEPT
CHAPELS
CHOIR
T
TS
STEPS
T
C
SANCTUARY
TS
TS
TS
BOOK PRESSES
SOUTH
TRANSEPT
CHAPELS
NIGHT-
STAIR
SLYPE
DRAIN
C
CHAPTER-HOUSE
C
VESTIBULE
OLD CHAPTER
HOUSE
DOOR
TO
DAY
STAIRS
WARMING
HOUSE
RERE-DORTER
OR
NECESSARIUM
SEWER

to Bishop de Landells (died 1385). This attribution however is doubtful. The 'Scotichronicon' records his burial place as 'in the floor in front of the vestibule door of the great church'. The matrix stone is of Tournai marble. Similar stones occur frequently in medieval churches throughout Scotland. They were imported from the continent in large numbers for use with commemorative floor brasses. A second lies between the piers of the southern quire range.

The quire piers, of which the bases remain, can be dated to about 1200. Dwarf walls were later built between them.

Of the massive crossing-piers which carried the central tower, as if on stilts, only the lower courses of the western remain. It is evident that they were strengthened by contracting the arches opening to nave and aisles and by filling in the eastern bays of the nave arcade on either side.

The South Transept

The southern respond of the south transept, where there were three eastern chapels, is all that remains of the arcade there. It is of early fifteenth-century date and was probably built during the reconstruction after the collapse of the transept gable in 1409. Opposite, in the south-west angle, is the night-stair leading from the monk's dormitory down to the ritual quire. The west wall of the transept stands almost intact to the wall-head. It is enriched with an interlaced arcade. Above is a series of stilted arches as a framework to the windows. Wall-shafts now vanished completed these features. Some of their bases remain.

There are several tombstones in the south transept. One commemorates Canon Roberth Cathall who died in 1380.

The west wall of the south transept showing interlaced arcading.

The Nave

The south side of the nave from the transept as far as the western processional door was completed in the Transitional period. Both sides of the south wall are divided into panels or bays, each containing a window set sufficiently high to clear the lean-to roof of the cloister walk. The corbels which carried that roof are for the most part *in situ.* In the four eastern bays the windows are round arched with high sloping sills. The windows of the six western bays were similar but the present twin-light pointed windows were inserted in the late thirteenth-century style, probably during the reconstruction by Bishop Wishart after the collapse of the west front. The two bays beyond the west processional doorway are later and were built at the end of the thirteenth century but before the present west front was erected. The lofty arched recesses which relieve otherwise plain walling are of no particular significance.

The south aisle, viewed from inside the church, showing the change of window design.

The processional doors are both blocked. The credence niche and *piscina* of the west side of the east door are late insertions. The western doorway was widened in the second quarter of the thirteenth

The west door and the nave.

century, when the existing segmental rear arch was constructed and a new pointed doorway with dog-tooth and nail-head enrichments was built on the outside. The present east jamb of the latter is largely modern. This doorway was subsequently contracted.

The south aisle was vaulted throughout in quadripartite vaulting. That this was planned from the beginning is proved by the late twelfth-century bases of the wall-shafts which are identical from the western processional door to the quire. In the two bays west of this door the wall-shafts have a fillet in the central member and rise to double-capitals from bases of water-holding type dating before 1273. As has been already stated, the church extended beyond the present west front and the wall-shafts of the discarded westernmost bays can still be seen. The later existing west end was built against one of them. It has been disclosed by the removal of a stone at the junction of the west end and the south wall. All these have a fillet on the central member and their bases are likewise similar to those of the two bays east of the entrance. Although the bases and shafts point to two principal building periods in the late twelfth and thirteenth centuries, the capitals indicate alteration and reconstruction corresponding to the alteration of the windows. The wall-shafts of the four eastern Transitional bays have tightly curled foliage capitals, whereas in the next six bays with later windows the shafts are of later type without capitals.

The West Front

The original west front was thrown down in a tempest and subsequently rebuilt in its present position by Bishop Wishart between 1273–79. The reconstruction was two bays east of its predecessor, thereby reducing the length of the nave by 10·36 m (34 ft) (excavations have revealed foundations beyond the west front). This contraction was probably made with the double purpose of avoiding the damaged walls of the two westernmost bays and of otherwise using them for the less dangerous construction of a porch or narthex.

The evidence of this remodelling can be clearly seen. The west end does not bond into the side walls. On each side of the doorway is the remains of a respond rising above the capitals. A similar shaft will be observed at the angle of the west front and the south wall. From them sprang the ribs of the vaulted porch, three bays wide by two deep, which extended across the front. Such a porch, called the Galilee, was common in France but unusual in England and Scotland.

This example was removed during the late fourteenth-century rebuilding after further damage by fire, when the upper part of the existing front was also reconstructed. A wall passage over the doorway was built. It had an open arcade to the interior. The arcade was removed and the wall built up solid. On the interior the existing blind-arcade was built up. It is similar to that of the Pends. The floor level of this passage was 90 cm (3 ft) above the string course upon which the external blind arcading now stands.

Hewn-off wall-ribs rise from the respond to this string course, and are elsewhere evident. About the middle of the last century a number of new stones were inserted in the west front and on some of those the obliterated traces of the wall-ribs are indicated by a shallow incision.

The entrance doorway is small in scale; the jambs are shafted, the shafts having water-holding bases and bell-shaped capitals on which remain traces of stiff-leaf foliage. On the south jamb is a much weathered head of a mitred ecclesiastic, probably a conventional portrait of Bishop Wishart.

Above the arcading surmounting the doorway were twin three-light windows

The west front of the cathedral.

with moulded jambs and geometric bar-tracery. Above them were two double-light windows of similar detail. They are contemporary with the arcading: the outer jambs were spliced into the masonry of the lofty turrets flanking the doorway. The upper part of the gable probably contained a large wheel-window.

The cloisters viewed from the chapter-house.

The Monastic Buildings

The monastic buildings were the domestic and office buildings of the priory and lay to the south of the church round the cloister. The **east range** abutted the south transept gable and contained in the ground floor a slype or passage leading to the monastic cemetery and probably to the infirmary but serving also as a 'parlour'. The entrance has a semi-circular head and jambs with attached shafts. The capitals of the shafts are enriched with pearl ornament. The passage had a bench along the walls. Above the bench remaining on the north side are traces of a Transitional interlaced arcade. A gutter is in the floor.

The **chapter-house** has a fine entrance and flanking windows of mid-thirteenth-century date. The piers between the doorway and the windows are of 'southern' type, having a cylinder for core and four detached shafts disclosed at the cardinal points. The capitals are roll-moulded and the bases slightly overhang the plinths upon which they rest. The arches are enriched with the nail-head ornament. The interior was originally a vaulted apartment of nine bays, three in width by three in depth. On the north wall can be seen the remains of benching and arcading.

Beyond this chamber, to the east, the second chapter-house was built, between 1313 and 1321. The original then became a vestibule or outer chapter-house. The communicating doorway between was most imposing. Four orders of attached shafts flanked the internal and external jamb of both sides and on either side was a lancet window. The second chapter-house had, like the first, benching and a blind arcade around the walls. The surviving arcade of the south wall, the 'curious seats' of Lamberton, is similar to that of the Pends and west front. The original chapter-house with its vaulted aisle plan is of the conventional Cistercian type, while the later is of the unaisled Benedictine form. Ecclesiastical dignitaries were frequently buried in the chapter-house.

Two stone coffins were found in the earlier chapter-house. They are thought to be the tombs of Prior John de Hadyngton (1304) and Prior John Machane (1313) who are recorded to have been buried here close to each other. In the later chapter-house five stone coffins and fragments of two others were discovered. John of Forfar (1321) 'was the first to be buried in the new chapter-house'. He was followed to the honoured resting place by John of Gowry (1340), William of Lothian (1354), Robert of Montrose (1393), and James Bisset (1416). The cemetery of the brethren lay to the east of the cloister, between the eastern limb of the church and the east cloister range of buildings.

South of the chapter-house is a chamber, once vaulted in three bays. The doorways to this and the day-stair adjacent are distinguished by carved heavy lintels of doubtful authenticity. That of the **day-stair** is less suspect as its moulded detail is of mid-thirteenth-century type, but its junction with the arched mouldings is awkward and ill-conceived and gives an impression of a secondary insertion. The jambs of this doorway are shafted. The shafts have moulded bases of the water-holding type and foliaceous capitals; indications of a disturbance are apparent, particularly at the south capital.

Access to the dorter or dormitory on the first floor during the day was by this stair, hence the name. Access from the dorter to the church was by the night-stair descending to the south transept. This was used by the brethren during the night services.

Beyond the day-stair is the **warming-house**, six bays long by two broad. It has two entrances, one in the west wall entering from a slype at the south end of the east cloister-walk, the other on the south wall from what was a covered way between the warming-house and the reredorter. The warming-house was so called as it contained the only fireplace common to the community. It is in the east wall. This chamber was largely reconstructed at the end of the last century.

In order to provide adequate sleeping accommodation for the monks whose dorter or dormitory extended over all the length of the apartments on the ground floor, the east range continued southwards beyond the south cloister range. It terminated with the **reredorter** (latrine) block which projects eastwards. The foundations of its vaulted basement remain with the bases of two of the central vaulting piers. Running deep along its south side is the great monastic drain of flowing water which served the dormitory latrines on the first floor.

Of the **south range** only the sub-croft remains. It also was constructed at the end of the last century. Above was the frater or refectory (dining hall). The rounded lower part of the refectory pulpit projects externally from the south wall.

The **western range** is represented only by dilapidated barrel-vaulted cellars of a late date and little importance.

In the wall of the church at the north end of this range some evidence remains of a cross-wing returning westwards as far as the original west end. This wing was vaulted in five bays on the ground floor and on the upper had a wall arcading. When the church was reduced in length the ground was re-vaulted in two bays.

Beyond the east range is an isolated building commonly called the **Prior's House.** It is a later building now restored and in use as a museum for gravestones of post-Reformation date.

Within the cloister are two deep **wells**;

another is in the nave of the church. That within the south cloister walk was the well of the 'lavatorium' where the monks washed before entering the refectory. Nearby would be a seemly oaken cupboard for clean towels. The purpose of the other two was to serve the needs of the masons engaged in the erection of the fabric.

The Pends and Precinct Wall

To the west of the cathedral stand the stately remains of the **entrance gateway** to the cathedral precinct, called the Pends. Only the outer shell of the building remains, with the wall springers of its vaulting. Above would be a porter's lodging. It dates from the fourteenth century. The area of the precinct was about 30 acres (12·14 hectares), surrounded by a wall 1·6 km long, 6·1 m (20 ft) high and 9 cm (3 ft) thick. The **precinct wall** was fortified by attached towers, some round and others square, disposed at intervals throughout its entire length. The towers are equipped with loops and embellished with niches and in some cases heraldic panels. These panels testify that the wall was constructed or reconstructed by Prior John Hepburn, who died in 1522, and his successor and nephew, Prior Patrick Hepburn, later bishop of Moray. The existence of the Pends in the fourteenth century implies no less certainly that the precinct was walled at that time and a careful scrutiny of the wall throughout its extent strengthens this inference. Half-way up its height there may be observed, particularly in the Abbey Walk stretch,

The Pends.

The arms of Prior Hepburn, dated to 1520.

indications of a change of masonry. It is not without significance that the aforesaid niches and panels of the towers are above this. It is therefore probable that the lower part of the wall is of fourteenth-century construction, only the upper part being of the sixteenth century.

The wall runs from the north-east buttress of the cathedral to a round tower; this stretch is of later origin. Thence it turns towards the harbour, follows the shore for some 274 m (300 yds), turns back up the Abbey Walk for some 400 m (440 yds) and thence returns towards the Pends. Facing the harbour at the end of the road from the Pends is the gateway known as the Sea Yett or Mill Port. Another gateway known as the Teinds Yett is in the Abbey Walk. Behind it were the Teinds Barns. It has one large entrance for cart traffic and a smaller for pedestrians. The six windows above lit the porter's lodging.

The cathedral and precincts as they might have been about 1550, drawn by Alan Sorrell in 1965.

Head of Christ from a life-size statue.

THE MUSEUM

The Museum
In the museum is a miscellany of relics associated with the cathedral. Of particular interest is the fine head of a Christ of thirteenth-century date and the two fragments of a bishop's effigy. The detached head of this effigy has long been in the museum. The other piece which shows the bottom of the chasuble was recovered during the demolition of a house in South Street, where it had been reused as a window lintel. It has carved upon it an armorial shield.

The collection of early Christian sculptured stones is of great interest and importance. More than fifty fragments of small cross-slabs were found in excavating the foundations of the church of St Mary of the Rock to the north of the cathedral overlooking the harbour; others were recovered nearby. They support the historical evidence of connection between St Andrews and Northumbria, in the eighth, ninth and tenth centuries. At this time St Andrews was the workshop of a notable school of imported or mixed Celtic-Anglian art, as shown by the various examples of Northumbrian or Anglian beasts, vine scrolls and interlacing plait designs. The small cross-slabs belong to the eighth and ninth centuries.

The shaft of a Celtic cross. This stone, and also the cross-slab illustrated on page 28—were built into the east gable of the cathedral and removed in 1909. The significance of the scenes on the cross-shaft is not known.

A 'rule-and-compass' cross-slab of the St Andrews workshop.

The blending of the Pictish and Anglian art forms is evident in the superb and unique sarcophagus which reveals also a possible eastern influence. Here we see representations of what may be David with the Lion, as a hunter, and as a shepherd or warrior. David was a prefiguration of Christ in Early Christian art and he is here represented in flowing draperies of unmistakably classical type. On this reading the sarcophagus may be dated to the eighth century. Should the figure struggling with the lion be a vivid illustration of the verse, 'He shall save me from the lion's mouth' and eastern derivations be rejected, the sacophagus may be attributed to the tenth century, on those and other technical considerations.

The sarcophagus, one of the finest examples of Dark Age art in Europe.

This tombstone of Helen Law, dated 1639, is one of a fine collection of post-medieval tombstones in the museum.

This seventeenth-century tombstone in the museum depicts death as a skeleton with a spear.

Glossary

Angle shaft a rounded shaft or column set in a recess
Barrel vault a continuous vault resembling a tunnel
Blind arcade decorative arcade on the face of a wall
Capital the carved top of a column
Chapter-house principal administrative office in a monastery, so called from the daily reading of a chapter from the Rule of the Order
Chases grooves
Clerestory or clear-storey the range of windows in the highest part of the church, admitting light
Corbel a projecting stone for the support of a timber beam or over-hanging wall
Day-stair day-time access to the dorter from the cloister walk
Dog-tooth a typical thirteenth-century ornamental feature in the form of a four-petalled flower with raised centre
Dorter dormitory
False arch straight lintel hollowed on under side to give appearance of an arch
Fillet a narrow raised band as part of a moulding
Loops apertures; usually for defence
Mid-shaft a column dividing a double window
Nail-head an ornament resembling a square nail-head
Night-stair access dorter to church; used by monks during the night services
Pilaster buttress a buttress with only a slight projection
Plinth the base of a wall or column
Processional doors two doors in south wall of the nave by which a monastic procession left and re-entered the church
Putlog hole an opening left in a wall for the insertion of a wooden beam
Quadripartite vault a vault divided into four panels by ribs
Quire choir
Quirk a sharp edged channel as part of the moulding
Raggle grooving in masonry to receive timber; especially on a wall for roof timbers
Reredorter the latrine block
Respond a half pillar attached to a wall: a wall support corresponding to a free-standing pier
Roll moulding a rounded moulding
Roll necking small rounded moulding on the neck of a capital
Sacristy or vestry the chamber wherein the vestments etc were kept
Slype passage
Springing or springers the lowest part of an arch or vault: the beginning of the curve
String-course a projecting moulding carried round a building
Sub-croft vaulted basement
Toothings remains of a wall projecting from an existing wall
Triforium the arcaded gallery between the main arcade and the clerestory
Voussoirs the wedge-shaped stones of an arch
Water-holding base a base with hollow mouldings; thirteenth-century

Printed by HMSO, Edinburgh Press
Dd 0762166 C95 5/86 (229788)